CW01024198

VEGAN PRESSURE COOKER COOKBOOK RECIPES

Quick and Easy Recipes Made Fast with Your Electric Pressure Cooker. 50+ Healthy Recipes for Living and Eating Well

Daniel Smith

Table of Contents

—

Introduction

 A healthy diet is key to having a happy, fulfilling life. A diet too full of unhealthy foods results in fatigue and vulnerability to diseases, many of them serious. Unfortunately, our society is not lacking in unhealthy options. To meet demand, companies turn to unethical methods, resulting in animal cruelty. Health and the treatment of animals are two of the main reasons why people commit to veganism, a plant-based diet that also eliminates animal products like milk, cheese, gelatin, and honey.

Getting the most nutrition out of every food is very important for vegans, and that's where pressure cooking shines. Pressure cookers are able to retain the most nutrition possible from vegetables and beans, and the appliance makes healthy cooking extremely easy. While there are packaged vegan options, making your own meals is always the healthy alternative, and much less expensive. This book presents the first steps in becoming a vegan, and provides 50 recipes for breakfasts, entrees, sides, desserts, and more, so you have a strong foundation to build off of.

Whether you're already a vegan and just need more recipe options, or have just started considering transitioning your diet, this book will give you everything you need to succeed.

Pear Oats with Walnuts

Serves: 4

Time: 6 minutes

Rolled oats are one of the fastest cooking foods with the pressure cooker. For this recipe, you mix everything in a bowl, which sets in the steamer rack in the cooker. The oats cook in almond milk, sugar, and just a tablespoon of coconut oil. Fresh pears will soften beautifully in there, as well, and you finish it off with cinnamon and walnuts.

Ingredients:

2 cups almond milk
2 cups peeled and cut pears
1 cup rolled oats
½ cup chopped walnuts
¼ cup sugar
1 tablespoon melted coconut oil
¼ teaspoon salt Dash of cinnamon

Directions:

1. Mix everything except the walnuts and cinnamon in an oven-safe bowl that you know fits in the pressure cooker.

2. Pour 1 cup of water into the pressure cooker and lower in steamer rack.

3. Put the bowl on top and lock the lid.

4. Select "manual," and then high pressure for 6 minutes.

5. When time is up, quick-release the pressure.

6. Carefully remove the bowl, divide into 4 servings, and season with salt and cinnamon.

Nutritional Info (¼ recipe):

Total calories: 288
Protein: 5
Carbs: 39
Fiber: 4.5
Fat: 13

Banana-Buckwheat Porridge (Oil Free)

Serves: 3-4

Time: 26 minutes (6 minutes cook time, 20 minutes natural release)

Buckwheat is a good oat-alternative if you're sensitive to gluten. It's also high in fiber and has comparable health benefits to fruits and veggies! Because of its texture, buckwheat takes a little longer to cook than rolled oats, so you need to do a natural pressure release to make sure it's soft enough.

Ingredients:

3 cups almond (or rice) milk
1 cup buckwheat groats
1 sliced banana
¼ cup raisins
1 teaspoon cinnamon
½ teaspoon pure vanilla extract

Directions:

1. Rinse off the buckwheat and put right in the pressure cooker.

2. Pour in the milk, and add the rest of the ingredients.

3. Lock the lid.

4. Select "manual," and then cook for 6 minutes on high pressure.

5. When time is up, hit "cancel" and wait 20 minutes or so for the pressure to go all the way down.

6. Open the lid and stir well. Add more milk if it's too thick for you.

7. Serve!

Nutritional Info (¼ recipe):

Total calories: 240
Protein: 6
Carbs: 46
Fiber: 5
Fat: 4

Pumpkin Spice Oatmeal w/ Brown Sugar Topping (Oil Free)

Serves: 6-8

Time: 15 minutes (3 minutes cook time, 12 minutes natural release)

If someone tells you that vegan food is bland, serve them this breakfast and they'll change their mind. It uses steel-cut oats, pumpkin puree, cinnamon, and allspice. The brown sugar, chopped pecan topping is just as delicious and adds a nice crunch.

Cooking Tip: If you like really soft oats, cook for at least 7 minutes instead of 3.

Ingredients:

4 ½ cups water
1 ½ cups steel-cut oats
1 ½ cups pumpkin puree

2 teaspoons cinnamon

1 teaspoon vanilla
1 teaspoon allspice
½ cup brown sugar
¼ cup chopped pecans 1 tablespoon cinnamon

Directions:

1. Pour 1 cup water into the pressure cooker.

2. Add everything from the first ingredient list (including rest of the water) into an oven-safe bowl and set in the steamer basket.

3. Lower basket into the pressure cooker and lock the lid.

4. Select "manual," and cook on high pressure for 3 minutes.

5. When time is up, hit "cancel" and wait for the pressure to come down on its own.

6. Mix the topping ingredients in a small bowl.

7. When you serve, sprinkle on top. If necessary, add a little almond milk to the oats.

Nutritional Info (⅛ recipe):

Total calories: 207
Protein: 4
Carbs: 38
Fiber: 4
Fat: 4

Chai-Spiced Oatmeal with Mango (Oil Free)

Serves: 2-3

Time: 13 minutes (3 minutes cook time, 10 minutes natural release)

A fan of chai tea? This oatmeal mimics those spicy-sweet flavors with cinnamon, ginger, cloves, and cardamom. The measurements are in "dashes," because it's up to you how much of each spice you want, depending on your tastes. Top the bowl off with some fresh-cut mango, or whatever fruit you like.

Cooking Tip: Cardamom and cloves are really strong, so add a teeny amount and taste.

Ingredients:

3 cups water
1 cup steel-cut oats
½ teaspoon vanilla
Dash of cinnamon
Dash of ginger Dash of cloves
Dash of cardamom
Dash of salt
½ mango, cut into pieces

Directions:

1. Mix water and oats in the pressure cooker.

2. Close the lid.

3. Select "manual," and cook for 3 minutes on high pressure.

---

4. When the beeper sounds, hit "cancel" and wait for the pressure to come down naturally.

5. Open the lid and stir well.

6. Season and taste.

7. Divide into even servings and add chopped mango.

Nutritional Info (⅓ recipe):

Total calories: 236
Protein: 6
Carbs: 44
Fiber: 5.5
Fat: 4

Coconut-Almond Risotto (Oil Free)

Serves: 4

Time: 20 minutes (10 minutes cook time, 10 minutes natural release)

Risotto is usually reserved for savory side dishes, but it's a perfect vehicle for sweeter breakfasts, too. Using vanilla almond milk and coconut milk adds flavor and a beautiful creaminess. For texture, a topping of coconut flakes and sliced almonds is perfect.

Ingredients:

2 cups vanilla almond milk
1 cup coconut milk
1 cup Arborio rice
⅓ cup sugar
2 teaspoons pure vanilla
¼ cup sliced almonds and coconut flakes

Directions:

1. Pour the milks into the pressure cooker and hit the "sauté" button.

2. Stir until it boils.

3. Add the rice and stir before locking the lid.

4. Select "manual," and cook for 5 minutes on high pressure.

5. When time is up, press "cancel" and wait 10 minutes. Quick-release any leftover pressure.

6. Add the sugar and vanilla.

7. Divide up oats and top with almonds and coconut.

Nutritional Info (¼ recipe):

Total calories: 337
Protein: 6 Carbs: 66
Fiber: 1.5
Fat: 7

Soy Yogurt (Oil Free)

Makes: 8 cups
Time: 12 hours to make + 6 hours in fridge before eating

Vegan yogurt? Yes, it's possible. It's a lot of waiting, but very little work. To make this recipe, you'll need an electric pressure cooker which has the Yogurt program. To ensure this yogurt is vegan, make sure to get a soymilk that only lists water and soybeans in the ingredients.

Ingredients:

2 quarts of soy milk
1 packet of vegan yogurt culture

Directions:

1. Mix milk and yogurt culture together.

2. Pour into a heatproof container that you know fit in your pressure cooker. Leave off any lids.

3. Put into the cooker. You do not need to add any water to the pot because it doesn't actually rise to pressure!

4. Close the lid and select the "yogurt" button. Adjust time to 12 hours for a professional-quality thick, creamy yogurt.

5. Go about your business until time is up, and then take out the yogurt.

6. Put the lids on the containers and store in the fridge for at least 6 hours.

7. The yogurt will be very tangy, so sweeten with vanilla, sugar, jam, fruit, and so on!

Nutritional Info (1 cup):

Total calories: 55
Protein: 4
Carbs: 5 Fiber: .5
Fat: 2

Banana-Amaranth Porridge (Oil Free)

Serves: 4

Time: 13 minutes (3 minutes cook time, 10 minutes natural release)

Amaranth is an ancient "grain," though it technically isn't a grain at all. It's basically a bud, but has similar health benefits to other cereals, and it makes a darn tasty hot porridge. This recipe uses no added sugar; bananas add the sweetness.

Ingredients:

2 ½ cups unsweetened almond milk

1 cup amaranth

2 sliced bananas

3 Dash of cinnamon

Directions:

1. Mix the amaranth, milk, and bananas in your pressure cooker.

2. Seal the lid.

3. Select "manual," and cook on high pressure for just 3 minutes.

4. When time is up, hit "cancel" and wait for the pressure to come down on its own.

5. When all the pressure is gone, you can serve the porridge with cinnamon.

Nutritional Info (¼ recipe):

Total calories: 271
Protein: 8
Carbs: 47
Fiber: 3.25
Fat: 6

Black Bean + Sweet Potato Hash (Oil Free)

Serves: 4

Time: About 15 minutes (5 minutes prep time, 10 minutes cook time)

Hashes make a great breakfast, because they're easy to make and easy to make nutritious. This one uses protein-heavy black beans and sweet potatoes. A little chili powder adds some heat to wake up even the sleepiest commuters.

Ingredients:

2 cups peeled, chopped sweet potatoes
1 cup chopped onion
1 cup cooked and drained black beans
1 minced garlic clove
⅓ cup veggie broth
¼ cup chopped scallions
2 teaspoons hot chili powder

Directions:

1. Prep your veggies.

2. Turn your pressure cooker to "sauté" and cook the chopped onion for 2-3 minutes, stirring so it doesn't burn.

3. Add the garlic and stir until fragrant.

4. Add the sweet potatoes and chili powder, and stir.

5. Pour in the broth and give one last stir before locking the lid.

6. Select "manual," and cook on high pressure for 3 minutes.

7. When time is up, quick-release the pressure carefully.

8. Add the black beans and scallions, and stir to heat everything up.

9. Season with salt and more chili powder if desired.

Nutritional Info (¼ recipe):

Total calories: 133
Protein: 5
Carbs: 28
Fiber: 9.5
Fat: 1

Cranberry-Walnut Quinoa (Oil Free)

Serves: 4

Time: 10 minutes

This breakfast bowl tastes like the holidays. You just cook up quinoa and mix in dried cranberries, chopped walnuts, and sunflower seeds. Add a favorite vegan sweetener and cinnamon.

Ingredients:

2 cups water
2 cups dried cranberries
1 cup quinoa
1 cup chopped walnuts
1 cup sunflower seeds ½ tablespoon cinnamon *Directions*:

1. Rinse quinoa.

2. Put quinoa, water, and salt in the pressure cooker.

3. Lock the lid.

4. Select "manual," and cook for 10 minutes on high pressure.

5. When the timer beeps, hit "cancel" and quick-release.

6. When the pressure is gone, open the cooker.

7. Mix in the dried cranberries, nuts, seeds, sweetener, and cinnamon.

8. Serve and enjoy!

Nutritional Info (¼ recipe):

Total calories: 611
Protein: 13
Carbs: 85
Fiber: 5.25
Fat: 29

Breakfast Tofu Scramble (Oil Free)

Serves: 4

Time: 9 minutes (5 minutes prep time, 4 minutes cook time)

Breakfast scrambles are quick, easy, and you can add just about anything you want. This recipe includes cherry tomatoes, a potato, and an apple. Instead of eggs, you use crumbled tofu. Seasonings are up to you, as well, and since tofu is pretty bland, don't be shy.

Ingredients:

1 block of extra-firm, crumbled tofu
1 cup cherry tomatoes
1 onion
1 diced potato
1 diced apple
¼ cup veggie broth
2 minced garlic cloves
1 teaspoon dry dill
½ teaspoon ground turmeric Salt and pepper to taste

Directions:

1. Turn your pressure cooker to sauté and dry-cook the garlic and onion until the onion begins to soften.

2. Add a bit of water if it starts to stick.

3. Pour broth into cooker, and add the rest of the ingredients.

4. Select "manual" and cook on high pressure for 4 minutes.

5. When time is up, hit "cancel" and quick-release.

6. Stir, season to taste, and enjoy!

Nutritional Info (¼ recipe):

Total calories: 139
Protein: 12
Carbs: 15
Fiber: 1
Fat: 5

Millet Bowl with Lentils and Sugar-Snap Peas (Oil Free)

Serves: 4

Time: 35 minutes (10 minutes prep time, 25 minutes cook time)

Millet is a tiny grain found in birdseed, but when you cook it in a pressure cooker, it expands into a nutty, fluffy dish similar to quinoa. Perfect for lunch or dinner, this bowl also includes sugar-snap peas, mushrooms, onions, and lentils.

Ingredients:

2 ¼ cups veggie stock
1 cup rinsed millet
1 cup sliced onion

1 cup sliced sugar snap peas

½ cup oyster mushrooms
½ cup rinsed green lentils
¼ cup chopped parsley

2 minced garlic cloves

Dash of lemon juice
Dash of salt

Directions:

1. Prep your ingredients.
2. Turn your pressure cooker to "sauté" and add garlic, onion, and mushrooms.
3. After 2 minutes, add the millet and lentils, and stir for 1 minute.
4. Pour in the stock.
5. Lock and seal the lid.
6. Select "manual," and then 10 minutes on high pressure.
7. When time is up, hit "cancel" and let the pressure come down on its own.
8. Pour in the peas and close the lid for a few minutes, without bringing to pressure, to heat everything through.
9. Stir and add the herbs.
10. Divide into bowls and squeeze some lemon juice on each serving.

Nutritional Info (¼ recipe):

Total calories: 230
Protein: 7
Carbs: 45
Fiber: 4.25
Fat: 2

Sweet Potato + Black-Eyed Pea Bowl

Serves: 4

Time: About 25 minutes (5 minutes prep time, 20 minutes cook time)

Sweet potatoes are hearty and a great vehicle for spices. For this bowl, the spices of choice include garlic, cumin, and coriander. For protein, you've got black-eyed peas, the pressure cooker cooks perfectly.

Ingredients:

3-4 halved sweet potatoes
1 ½ cups water

2 cups spinach

1 cup rinsed black-eyed peas
1 chopped onion
4 smashed garlic cloves
1 tablespoon olive oil
1 tablespoon tomato paste
1 teaspoon cumin seeds
½ teaspoon coriander seeds
Dash of salt

Directions:

1. Prep your ingredients.
2. Put the potatoes (cut-side up) in the steamer basket.
3. Hit "sauté" on your pressure cooker and add olive oil.
4. When hot, sauté onion.
5. When the onion is soft, add garlic and cool for a minute.
6. Add black-eyed peas, water, and tomato paste, and stir.
7. Lower in the steamer basket with potatoes.
8. Lock and seal the lid.
9. Select "manual," and cook for 12 minutes on high pressure.
10. When time is up, quick-release the pressure.
11. Take out the potatoes.
12. Add spinach to the cooker and a dash of salt, and let the leaves wilt.
13. Serve, with two potato halves per guest!

Nutritional Info (¼ recipe):

Total calories: 273.6
Protein: 8.2
Carbs: 48.5
Fiber: 9.8
Fat: 6.3

Red Curry + Sweet Potato Bowl (Oil Free)

Serves: 4-6

Time: About 20 minutes (5 minutes prep time, 20 minutes natural release)

Are you hungry for a spicy, veggie-full bowl of goodness that will warm you on cool nights? This lentil-and-sweet potato bowl is flavored with Thai red curry paste, so you don't have to mess with a lot of expensive whole spices.
That heat is mellowed out with coconut milk.

Ingredients:

1 pound peeled and cubed sweet potatoes
1 ¾ cups veggie stock
1 large chopped onion
4 minced garlic cloves
1 cup cauliflower florets
½ cup green lentils
½ cup coconut milk
1 tablespoon lime juice
 2 teaspoons Thai red curry paste

Directions:

1. Prep your ingredients.

2. Turn your pressure cooker to "sauté" and cook the onion for about 1 minute.

3. Add garlic and cook for another minute.

4. Add ¾ cup veggie stock, lentils, curry paste, and coconut milk.

5. Close and seal the lid.

6. Choose "manual," and then cook for 3 minutes on high pressure.

7. When time is up, hit "cancel" and let the pressure come down by itself.

8. Add, cubed potato and 1 cup of stock.

9. Close the lid again and seal.

10. Select "manual" again, and cook for 10 minutes.

11. When the timer beeps, quick-release the pressure this time.

12. Add broccoli and close the lid to let the leftover heat cook the broccoli.

13. Season and serve!

Nutritional Info (¼ recipe):

Total calories: 201
Protein: 7
Carbs: 38
Fat: 5
Fiber: 5.5

Tofu, Kale, and Sweet Potato Bowl

Serves: 2-4

Time: Under 10 minutes (3 minutes cook time)

Tofu is the perfect vehicle for all sorts of flavors. It's like a taste sponge, and for this recipe, it's absorbing flavors from onion, fresh garlic, ginger, and cayenne pepper. Sweet potatoes and kale leaves add body, sweetness, and antioxidants.

Ingredients:

1 peeled and cut sweet potato

2 cups sliced kale leaves (stems and ribs removed)

8 ounces cubed tofu

1 chopped onion

2 minced garlic cloves

¼-½ cup veggie broth
1-3 teaspoons tamari
1 teaspoon ground ginger
½ teaspoon ground cayenne
1 teaspoon olive oil Squeeze of lemon juice
Directions:

1. After prepping your ingredients, turn your pressure cooker to "sauté" and add oil.

2. When hot, sauté the tofu for a minute.

3. Mix in the tamari with a few tablespoons of broth.

4. Stir for a minute.

5. Add sweet potatoes, onion, garlic, and the rest of the broth.

6. Select "manual," and cook on high pressure for 2 minutes.

7. When time is up, hit "cancel" and quick-release.

8. Throw in the kale and seal back up for another 1 minute on high pressure.

9. Quick-release.

10. Divide up the meal and serve with a squirt of fresh lemon.

Nutritional Info (¼ recipe):

Total calories: 133
Protein: 11 Carbs: 13
Fiber: 2.25
Fat: 5

Mexican Casserole (Oil Free)

Serves: 4

Time: 28 minutes (+ 2-hours soak time for beans)

Get ready to make the easiest casserole ever. You just need rice, beans, tomato paste, and a few spices. It's a great option for when you're trying to put off going to the store, but you don't want to eat a dinner of crackers and peanut butter.

Ingredients:

5 cups water
2 cups uncooked brown rice

1 cup soaked black beans

6-ounces tomato paste

2 teaspoons chili powder

2 teaspoons onion powder
1 teaspoon garlic
1 teaspoon salt

Directions:

1. A few hours before dinner, put your dry beans in a bowl with enough water to cover them.

2. Soak on the countertop for at least two hours and drain.

3. Put everything in your pressure cooker.

4. Close and seal the cooker.

5. Select "manual," and then cook on high pressure for 28 minutes.

6. When time is up, hit "cancel" and quick-release.

7. Taste and season more if necessary.

Nutritional Info (¼ recipe):

Total calories: 322
Protein: 6
Carbs: 63
Fiber: 9
Fat: 2

Black-Eyed Pea Masala (Oil Free)

Serves: 8

Time: 1 hour, 30 minutes (1 hour for bean prep, 7 minutes cook time, 20 minutes natural release)

This classic Indian dish usually has a "chicken" before the "masala," but to veganize it, you use black-eyed peas instead. To cut down on time, you can quick-soak the beans by boiling them for 1 minute, and then letting them sit for at least 1 hour. Garam masala is a spice mix you can get just about anywhere.

Ingredients:

2 cups water
2 cups dried black-eyed peas
2, 15-ounce cans of diced tomato
1 diced onion
1 tablespoon minced garlic
1 tablespoon ginger paste

2 teaspoons garam masala

2 teaspoons cumin seeds
1 teaspoon sugar
1 teaspoon turmeric
1 teaspoon salt ½ teaspoon cayenne

Directions:

1. To quick-soak the beans, boil for 1 minute and then let them sit for at least 1 hour.

2. Preheat your pressure cooker and add a tiny bit of oil.

3. Add the onions and cook until they're soft.

4. Add cumin seeds and cook for 1 minute before adding ginger and garlic.

5. Drain the beans and add to the pot, along with the rest of the ingredients.

6. Close and seal the lid.

7. Select "manual," and cook for 7 minutes on high pressure.

8. When time is up, hit "cancel" and wait for the pressure to come down on its own.

9. Season.

10. Check the peas, and if they aren't tender enough, simmer for a little while.

Nutritional Info (⅛ recipe):

Total calories: 178
Protein: 11
Carbs: 32.8
Fiber: 5.8
Fat: 0

Italian Tofu Scramble

Serves: 4

Time: 12 minutes (5 minutes prep time, 7 minutes cook time)

This one-pot scramble is vegan Italy in a bowl. It's got garlic, tomatoes, Italian seasoning, and crumbled tofu, which takes on an egg-like texture. It only takes four minutes to cook, and then a quick-release.

Ingredients:

3 minced garlic cloves
1 sliced onion
1 cup diced carrots
1 block of extra firm tofu

1 can Italian-style diced tomatoes

¼ cup veggie broth

2 tablespoons jarred banana pepper rings

1 tablespoon Italian seasoning
1 teaspoon olive oil
1 teaspoon cumin Ground black pepper

Directions:

1. Heat the olive oil in your pressure cooker on "sauté."

2. Add garlic, onion, and carrot for three minutes until the veggies are softened.

3. Crumble the tofu into the pot.

4. Pour in veggie broth, peppers, tomatoes, and seasoning.

5. Mix before locking and sealing the lid.

6. Select "manual" and cook for 4 minutes on high pressure.

7. When time is up, hit "cancel" and quick-release.

8. Taste and season before serving.

Nutritional Info (¼ recipe):

Total calories: 135
Protein: 11
Carbs: 11
Fiber: 1
Fat: 7

Sweet Potato Spinach Curry w/ Chickpeas

Serves: 2

Time: 15 minutes (5 minutes prep time, 8-10 minutes cook time)

Chickpeas are a vegan superfood. They are packed with nutrition, including fiber and protein, and have a hearty texture. When paired with sweet potatoes, you get a very filling dinner bowl spiced with red onion, ginger, garam masala, and cinnamon.

Ingredients:

1 small can of drained chickpeas
1 ½ cups chopped sweet potatoes
3 chopped garlic cloves
2 cups chopped fresh spinach
1 ½ cups water

2 chopped tomatoes

½ chopped red onion
½-inch thumb of ginger, chopped
1 teaspoon olive oil
1 teaspoon coriander powder
½ teaspoon garam masala
¼ teaspoon cinnamon
Salt and
pepper to
taste
Squeeze
of lemon

Directions:
    1 Pour oil in your pressure cooker and heat on "sauté." 2. When the oil is hot, add the ginger, onion, and garlic.

3.   When the onions are clear, add the spices and mix.

4.   After 30 seconds, add tomatoes and mix to coat everything.

5.   Add sweet potatoes, chickpeas, 1 ½ cups water, and a dash of salt.

6.   Close and seal the lid.

7.   Select "manual," and cook on high pressure for 8-10 minutes.

8.   When time is up, hit "cancel" and do a natural pressure release.

9.   Add the fresh spinach and stir so the heat wilts the leaves.

10.   Taste and season more if necessary.

11.   Serve with a squirt of fresh lemon.

Nutritional Info (½ recipe):

Total calories: 166.5
Protein: 6.8
Carbs: 32
Fiber: 7
Fat: 21

Easy Seitan Roast

Serves: 4

Time: 30 minutes (5 minutes prep time, 25 minutes cook time)

Seitan is a vegan meat substitute made from wheat gluten. It can be seasoned in a variety of ways, so you get rich flavors. This recipe uses plenty of herbs and salty ingredients. If you're gluten-intolerant or sensitive, stick to tofu, but if you aren't, try out this seitan roast in a flavorful simmering broth. You can pair seitan with any kind of vegan-friendly sauce or side.

Cooking Tip: When you slice seitan, it should have a meaty texture - not too soft, and not too chewy.

Ingredients:

1 ½ cups vital wheat gluten
1 cup veggie broth
⅓ cup tapioca flour
3 tablespoons nutritional yeast
2 tablespoons coconut aminos
1 tablespoon olive oil
1 tablespoon vegan Worcestershire sauce
1 teaspoon garlic powder
½ teaspoon dried thyme
½ teaspoon dried rosemary
¼ teaspoon black pepper
¼ teaspoon sea salt
3 cups veggie broth
2 cups water
¼ cup coconut aminos
2 tablespoons vegan Worcestershire
1 teaspoon onion powder

Directions:

1. Let's start with the first list of ingredients.
2. Whisk all the dry ingredients together.
3. In a separate bowl, mix the wet ones.
4. Pour the wet into the dry.
5. Fold first with a spoon, and then knead by hand for a few minutes.
6. Form into a round shape, pulling at the top, and then rolling under so it's smooth.
7. Shape into a more oblong loaf and roll tightly in cheesecloth, tying off the ends.
8. Put the roast in your pressure cooker.
9. Pour in all the ingredients in the second ingredient list.
10. Lock and seal the lid.
11. Select "manual," and cook on high pressure for 25 minutes.
12. When time is up, hit "cancel" and wait 10 minutes before quickreleasing the pressure.
13. Slice and serve!

Nutritional Info (¼ recipe):

Total calories: 451
Protein: 42
Carbs: 51
Fiber: 0
Fat: 4

Veggie Biryani

Serves: 8

Time: 30 minutes (15 minutes prep time, 15 minutes cook time)

Biryani is one of the most popular dishes in India. It's made from rice, and since so many people in India are vegetarian, many variations are vegetablebased. This particular biryani has cauliflower, potatoes, green beans, and carrots.

Ingredients:

2 cups rice
1 ½ cups water
1 ½ cups coconut milk
1 thinly-sliced onion
5 minced garlic cloves
1-inch thumb of ginger, grated
3 chopped small potatoes
1 small cauliflower's worth of florets
1 chopped carrot
1 cup green beans
¼ cup chopped mint leaves
¼ cup French's fried onions
1 tablespoon garam masala
1 tablespoon coconut oil
½ lemon, juiced

Directions:

1. Turn your pressure cooker to "sauté" and heat the oil.

2. When hot, add onion and mint leaves, and cook until the onions start to turn golden.

3. Add garlic and ginger.

4. After a minute, add the veggies and stir.

5. After 3 minutes, add fried onions.

6. Add the garam masala and coconut milk.

7. Pour in water and plenty of salt.

8. Lastly, add rice and lemon juice.

9. Mix everything before closing and sealing the lid.

10. Select "manual," and cook on high pressure for 3 minutes.

11. Hit "cancel" when time is up and wait for a natural release.

12. Stir with a fork before serving.

Nutritional Info (⅛ recipe):
Total calories: 215
Protein: 5
Carbs: 37
Fiber: 5.5
Fat: 6

Easy Ratatouille

Serves: 4

Time: 35 minutes (15 minutes prep time, 20 minutes cook time)

Ratatouille isn't just the name of a Pixar movie. It's a rustic eggplant dish originally from France; it's a vegan comfort food dream. There's also butternut squash, tomatoes, bell peppers, and plenty of garlic.

Ingredients:

3 cups diced butternut squash
2 cups chopped eggplant
4 chopped tomatoes
3 minced garlic cloves
2 chopped onions
1 chopped red bell pepper
1 chopped green bell pepper

1 tablespoon olive oil

2 teaspoons dried basil

1 teaspoon salt
½ teaspoon dried thyme ½ teaspoon black pepper

Directions:

1. Preheat your pressure cooker on the "sauté" setting and add oil.

2. When the oil is hot, cook the onion and garlic.

3. Add all your veggies, except tomatoes, and cook until they're soft.

4. Now you add the tomatoes.

5. Close and seal the pressure cooker lid.

6. Select "manual," and then five minutes on high pressure.

7. When time is up, hit "cancel" and let the pressure come down on its own.

8. Season and enjoy!

Nutritional Info (¼ recipe):

Total calories: 224
Protein: 9
Carbs: 38.2
Fiber: 8.6
Fat: 5.4

Jackfruit Sandwich "Meat"

Serves: 4

Time: 26 minutes (3 minutes prep time, 3 minutes cook time, 20 minutes release time)

You've heard of tempeh, tofu, and seitan as meat substitutes, but what about jackfruit? It has a very similar texture to meat, and when flavored with ingredients like cayenne, mustard seeds, garlic, and Worcestershire, it actually tastes a lot like the real thing! With this recipe, you can turn jackfruit into the perfect filling for BBQ sandwiches.

Ingredients:

17-ounces of rinsed and drained jackfruit (packed in water)
½-¾ cup water
¼ cup diced onion
3 tablespoons tomato paste 1 tablespoon minced garlic
1 tablespoon maple syrup
1 teaspoon olive oil
1 teaspoon apple cider vinegar
1 teaspoon vegan Worcestershire sauce
½ teaspoon cayenne pepper
½ teaspoon yellow mustard seeds
½ teaspoon salt
½ teaspoon black pepper

Directions:

1. Turn your pressure cooker to "sauté" and heat the oil.

2. When hot, add garlic and onion.

3. Cook for 3 minutes, or until the onion is soft.

4. Add the jackfruit, tomato paste, vinegar, Worcestershire, syrup, and seasonings.

5. Add just enough water to cover the jackfruit, and mix.

6. Close and seal the pressure cooker.

7. Select "manual," and cook on high pressure for 3 minutes.

8. Hit "cancel" when the timer goes off, and let the pressure come down naturally.

9. Open the lid and stir well.

10. With a fork, shred the fruit and serve on a toasted bun!

Nutritional Info (¼ recipe, jackfruit only):

Total calories: 79
Protein: 2
Carbs: 15
Fiber: 6
Fat: 1

Pressure-Cooker Penne Pasta

Serves: 2-4

Time: 25 minutes (5 minutes prep time, 20 minutes cook time)

Pressure cooking a pasta dinner is fast, but tastes like it's been simmering for hours. With a flavor base made from garlic, mushrooms, zucchini, onion, shallot, and herbs, the pasta cooks right in a homemade sauce.

Ingredients:

450 grams of penne pasta
3 minced garlic cloves
12 sliced white mushrooms
1 sliced zucchini
1 small sliced onion

1 small diced shallot

Pinch of dried oregano
Pinch of dried basil
Olive oil
Salt and pepper

2 cups water

1 cup veggie stock

Dash of sherry wine
½ cup tomato paste

2 tablespoons vegan-friendly light soy sauce

Directions:

1   Turn your pressure cooker to "sauté" to preheat the cooker.

2   Add oil and cook the shallot and onion.

3   Add salt and black pepper.

4   Stir until the veggies are browning.

5   Add the garlic and stir for half a minute.

6   Toss in the mushrooms, zucchini, and herbs.

7   Cook for a minute.

8   Time to make the sauce. Deglaze the pot with sherry.

9   Pour in veggie stock, 2 cups water, and soy sauce.

10   Put the pasta in the pot and mix in tomato paste so it's totally covered.

11   Select "manual" and cook for 4 minutes on high pressure.

12   When time is up, hit "cancel" and wait 5 minutes before quickreleasing the pressure.

13   Mix and serve!

Tip: Deglazing is when you add a cooking liquid (like water, broth, or wine) to a pot and scrape off the bits of food that have stuck to the sides. These burned or browned bits add flavor.

Nutritional Info (¼ recipe):

Total calories: 235
Protein: 11
Carbs: 49
Fiber: 5
Fat: 1

Sun-Dried Tomato Pesto Pasta w/ Chard

Serves: 4

Time: 17 minutes (10 minutes prep time, 7 minutes cook time)

Sundried tomato pesto is bright and goes perfectly with chard, which is similar to spinach. Dill and red pepper flakes add complexity and heat. To make the dish healthier, go with whole-wheat pasta.

Ingredients:

1 pound whole-wheat elbow macaroni
4 sliced garlic cloves
3 minced garlic cloves
8 sun-dried tomatoes
6 thinly-sliced Swiss chard leaves
¼ cup walnuts
¼ cup + 1 teaspoon olive oil
¼ cup dill
1 teaspoon red pepper flakes
½ lemon, juiced Salt to taste

Directions:

1. Put the tomatoes, dill, walnuts, minced garlic, ¼ cup olive oil, red pepper, lemon juice, and salt in a food processor.

2. Run until you get a rough paste.

3. Heat 1 teaspoon olive oil in your pressure cooker.

4. Add the sliced garlic and cook until they're golden.

5. Cook the chard until it wilts and the water is evaporated.

---

6. Add pasta and stir.

7. Pour in just enough water, so the pasta is covered.

8. Salt.

9. Close and seal the cooker. Select "manual," and cook on high pressure for 3 minutes.

10. When time is up, hit "cancel," and let the pressure come down naturally.

11. When all the pressure is gone, add the pesto and stir well.

12. Season to taste.

13. Serve!

Nutritional Info (¼ recipe):

Total calories: 334
Protein: 9
Carbs: 37
Fiber: 6
Fat: 19

Black-Eyed Pea Cakes (Oil Free)

Serves: 4

Time: 1 hour, 40 minutes (1 hour soak time for peas, 10 minutes prep time, 30 minutes cook time)

These Nigerian savory cakes make an awesome light lunch and pack a whopping 29 grams of protein per 2-cake serving. These patties are made from black-eyed peas, onion, roasted red pepper, and spiced with Old Bay seasoning. These need to be steamed, so you'll be using the "Steam" program on your pressure cooker.

Ingredients:

1 cup dried black-eyed peas
1 chopped onion
1 roasted red pepper
¼ cup veggie broth
1 tablespoon tomato paste
1 ½ - 2 teaspoons Old Bay seasoning
1 teaspoon salt ¼ teaspoon white pepper

Directions:

1. Rinse and pick over the peas to take out any stones.

2. Soak in a large bowl of hot water, so there's two inches about the peas.

3. Soak for one hour and then drain.

4. Put the peas in a food processor and pulse until they're just broken.

5. Put the peas in the bowl and cover with more water.

6. Rub them, so their skins come off.

7. With the skins gone, the peas are white.

---

8. Put the peas back into the food processor with the onion, red pepper, tomato paste, and 2 tablespoons of broth.

9. Process until smooth.

10. Pour into bowl and add seasonings.

11. You want the mixture to be thick, but still pourable. Add more broth if necessary.

12. Pour 1 cup of water into your pressure cooker.

13. Grease 8 ramekins and pour ½ of the cake batter into each one.

14. Wrap in foil.

15. Lower the steamer basket (or trivet) into the cooker, and place the ramekins inside.

16. Close and seal lid.

17. Select the "steam" program and adjust time to 30 minutes.

18. When time is up, hit "cancel" and quick-release.

19. With a toothpick, check the cakes - a clean toothpick means they're ready.

Nutritional Info (2 cakes):

Total calories: 158
Protein: 29
Carbs: 9
Fiber: 5
Fat: 1

Vegan Mac + Cheese

Serves: 2

Time: 20 minutes (15 minutes prep time, 5 minutes cook time)

One of the foods vegans miss most is cheese. Luckily, vegan cheese is a thing, as is vegan butter. Chicken seasoning, a spice blend made with rosemary, thyme, paprika, and so on, adds a ton of flavor, so don't skip it!

Ingredients:

1 cup whole-wheat elbow pasta

1 cup diced onion

2 minced garlic cloves

2 tablespoons chicken seasoning
2 tablespoons vegan butter
2 tablespoons nutritional yeast
2-ounces
shredded vegan
cheese Salt and
ground pepper
to taste

Directions:

1. Put the vegan butter in your pressure cooker and melt on "sautè."

2. Add the onion and garlic, and cook until the onion is clear.

3. Add the soy curls and chicken seasoning, and cook for 5 minutes.

4. Pour in the pasta, 2 cups of cool water, and nutritional yeast, and stir.

5. Select "manual," and cook on low pressure for 5 minutes, or high pressure for 3 minutes.

6. When time is up, hit "cancel" and quick-release the pressure. Stir and stir in vegan cheese, salt, and pepper.

7. Before serving, let the mac 'n cheese sit for about 5 minutes.

Nutritional Info (½ recipe):

Total calories: 352
Protein: 10
Carbs: 42
Fiber: 4.5
Fat: 18

Veggie-Quinoa Soup (Oil Free)

Serves: 6

Time: 20-40 minutes (2 minutes cook time, 20 minutes natural release)

This is the easiest soup you'll ever make. You literally just throw everything in the pressure cooker and step back. The quinoa adds a different flavor and consistency than the usual noodles

Cooking Tip: The reason the time range is so wide is because it can take between 15-20 minutes for the pressure cooker to reach pressure if you're using frozen veggies. Using boiling water helps with that, and if you use fresh veggies, it takes very little time to get to pressure)

Ingredients:

3 cups boiling water
2 bags of frozen mixed veggies (12-ounces each)
1 15-ounce can of white beans
1 15-ounce can of fire-roasted diced tomatoes
1 15-ounce can of pinto beans
¼ cup rinsed quinoa
1 tablespoon dried basil
1 tablespoon minced garlic
1 tablespoon hot sauce
½ tablespoon dried oregano
Dash of salt
Dash of black pepper

Directions:

1.   Put everything in the pressure cooker and stir.

2.   Close and seal the lid.

3.   Select "manual," and set time to 2 minutes on high pressure.

4.   When time is up, hit "cancel" and quick-release the pressure.

5.   When all the pressure is gone, open the cooker and season to taste.

6.   Serve!

Nutritional Info (1 ½ cups serving):

Total calories: 201
Protein: 11
Carbs: 37
Fiber: 11
Fat: 1.1

Turkish Soup

Serves: 1-2

Time: About 15 minutes (5 minutes prep time, 10 minutes cook time)

This simple soup has just the right amount of spices without being overwhelming for those with most delicate palates. It's thick and rich, but not too hearty. It would be a great option for lunch.

Ingredients:

1 cup red lentils
1 chopped carrot
1 chopped potato
1 chopped onion
½ cup celery
3 minced garlic cloves
½ tablespoon rice
3 teaspoons olive oil
½ teaspoon paprika
½ teaspoon coriander Salt to taste

Directions:

1. Turn your pressure cooker to "sauté" and add oil.

2. While that heats up, prep your veggies.

3. When oil is hot, cook the garlic for a few minutes until fragrant.

4. Rinse off the rice and lentils, and put them in the pressure cooker.

5. Add 2 ½ cups of water, paprika, salt, and veggies.

6. Close and seal the lid.

7. Select "manual" and cook on high pressure for 10 minutes.

8. When time is up, hit "cancel," and quick-release.

9. Let the mixture cool for a little while before pureeing in a blender.

10. Serve!

Nutritional Info (½ recipe):

Total calories: 531
Protein: 29
Carbs: 73
Fiber: 10
Fat: 9

Lentil Soup with Cumin and Coriander

Serves: 8

Time: 30 minutes (10 minutes prep time, 20 minutes cook time)

If you need a hot meal for a crowd, try out this lentil soup spiced with cumin and coriander. You can use brown or green lentils (I use brown), and you only need a few good veggies (potatoes, carrots, onion, and celery) to add tons of depth and flavor.

Ingredients:

8 cups of veggie broth
2 cups uncooked brown lentils
2 sliced carrots
2 cubed big Yukon gold potatoes
2 bay leaves
2 minced garlic cloves
1 chopped onion
1 chopped celery rib
1 teaspoon ground coriander
1/2
teaspoon
ground
cumin
Black
pepper to
taste

Directions:

1. First, pick through the lentils and throw out any stones, and then rinse.

2. Pour the broth in your pressure cooker and turn to "sauté" so it heats up.

3. Prep the veggies.

4. Add to the pressure cooker, along with everything else.

5. Close and seal the pressure cooker.

6. Select "manual," and cook on high pressure for 10 minutes.

7. After hitting "cancel," wait for 5 minutes before quick-releasing.

8. Check the tenderness of the lentils and potatoes.

9. If not done, turn the pot back on "sauté" and finish cooking with the lid on, but not sealed or at pressure.

10. Pick out the bay leaves, and salt to taste.

11. Serve with a squirt of lemon juice.

Nutritional Info (⅛ recipe):

Total calories: 228
Protein: 14.4
Carbs: 41
Fiber: 17
Fat: 0

Miso Soup

Serves: 4

Time: About 6 minutes

A lot of these recipes are Indian, because of the pressure cooker's popularity, so if you want to shake things up a bit, let's travel over to Japan. Miso soup is awesome for when you're feeling blue in the dead of winter. It's like a vegan's chicken noodle soup for the soul.

Cooking Tip: Wakame flakes are dehydrated type of seaweed, and can be found on Amazon or your local Asian market.

Ingredients:

4 cups water
1 cup cubed silken tofu2 chopped carrots

2 chopped celery stalks

1 sliced onion

2 tablespoons miso pasteDash of vegan-friendly soy sauce

Directions:

1. Put the carrots, onion, celery, tofu, wakame, and water in your pressure cooker.

2. Close and seal.

3. Select "manual," and cook on high pressure for 6 minutes.

4. When time is up, hit "cancel" and quick-release.

5. Open the lid and ladle out one cup of broth.

6. Add the miso paste to this broth and whisk until completely dissolved.

7. Pour back into pot and stir.

8. Season with soy sauce and serve!

Nutritional Info (¼ recipe):

Total calories: 74
Protein: 4
Carbs: 9
Fiber: 1
Fat: 2

Barley + Winter Vegetable Soup

Serves: 6-8

Time: About 25 minutes (5 minutes prep time, 8 minutes cook time, 10 minutes natural release)

For a hearty soup using in-season ingredients, you can't beat barley and winter veggies. Winter veggie options include turnips, sweet potato, rutabaga, or celery root. This recipe makes up to 8 servings, so you can eat it all week.

Ingredients:

6 cups veggie broth
1-3 cups water
2 cups chopped winter veggie
1 ½ cups chopped carrots
1 cup sliced onions
1 cup peeled, chopped parsnip
1 cup pearled barley

1 chopped potato

½ cup chopped celery
1-2 tablespoons tamari
1 tablespoon olive oil

1   tablespoon miso (dissolved in 3 tablespoons water)

Salt and pepper to taste

Directions:

1. oil into your pressure cooker and heat on the "sauté" setting
2. When hot, cook celery, carrots, and onions until the onions are browning.
3. Pour in the broth, and add potato, tamari, parsnip, and barley.
4. Close and seal the lid.
5. Select "manual" and cook on high pressure for 8 minutes.
6. When time is up, hit "cancel" and let the pressure come down naturally.
7. Check the barley, and if it isn't cooked through, bring the pot back to pressure for 3-5 minutes.
8. When ready, add the miso (dissolved in water).
9. Season and serve!

Nutritional Info (⅛ recipe):

Total calories: 233
Protein: 4
Carbs: 29
Fiber: 7
Fat: 2

Split-Pea Soup

Serves: 6

Time: 55 minutes (10 minutes prep time, 45 minutes cook time)

Split peas are commonly-paired with ham, but to veganize the classic soup, you use spices like smoked paprika, thyme, black pepper, and a bay leaf.
Other aromatics like celery, carrots, and onion add even more flavor.

Ingredients:

6 cups veggie broth
1 pound of split peas
3 diced carrots
3 diced celery ribs

1 diced yellow onion

2 minced garlic cloves

2 tablespoons coconut oil
1 bay leaf
½ tablespoon smoked paprika
¼ teaspoon dried thyme
Black pepper

Directions:

1. Prep your veggies.

2. Put everything in your pressure cooker and seal the lid.

3. Select "manual," then cook on high pressure for 15 minutes.

4. Hit "cancel" when time is up, and wait for the pressure to come down

   on its own.

5. When the pressure is gone, open and stir the soup.

6. Season to taste.

Nutritional Info (⅙ recipe):

Total calories: 180
Protein: 12
Carbs: 32
Fiber: 13
Fat: 1

Mexican Baked Potato Soup (Oil Free)

Serves: 4

Time: 35 minutes (5 minutes prep time, 10 minutes cook time, 20 minutes natural release)

Baked potatoes are great, but they can get a bit boring after a while. How about you turn them into a creamy soup? Just add veggie broth, a few extra ingredients like salsa and jalapenos, and season it all with garlic, cumin, and oregano, and you've got a delicious hot meal that's vegan and oil-free!

Ingredients:

4 cups veggie broth
4 cups diced potatoes
4 diced garlic cloves
1 diced onion
½ cup salsa
½ cup nutritional yeast
⅛ cup seeded jalapeno peppers
1 teaspoon cumin
¼ teaspoon oregano Black pepper to taste

Directions:

1. Turn your pressure cooker to "sauté." 2. When hot, add the onion, jalapeno, and garlic.

3. Stir until browning.

4. Hit "cancel" before adding potatoes, salsa, cumin, and oregano, and pouring the broth over everything.

5. Stir.

6. Close and seal the lid.

7. Select "manual," and cook for 10 minutes on high pressure.

8. When time is up, hit "cancel" and wait for the pressure to come down on its own.

9. After 20 minutes, release any leftover pressure.

10. To make the soup creamy, run through a blender.

11. Add nutritional yeast and pepper.

12. Serve!

Nutritional Info (¼ recipe):

Total calories: 196
Protein: 10
Carbs: 30
Fiber: 4
Fat: 0

Red Curry-Coconut Milk Soup (Oil Free)

Serves: 4

Time: 21 minutes (5 minutes prep time, 6 minutes cook time, 10 minutes natural release)

The heat from this recipe's red curry paste and red pepper is smoothed out with coconut milk, which also makes this soup creamy and lovely. Red lentils and spinach add a ton of nutritional value, and if there are leftovers, the soup freezes well for future meals to come.

Ingredients:

2 cups veggie broth
1 ½ cups red lentils
1, 15-ounce can of coconut milk
1, 14-ounce can of diced tomatoes (with liquid)
1 diced onion
3 minced garlic cloves
2 tablespoons red curry paste
⅛ teaspoon ground ginger
Dash of red pepper Handful of spinach

Directions:

1. Preheat your pressure cooker on the "sauté" setting.

2. When hot, cook onion and garlic until they're beginning to brown.

3. Hit "cancel."

4. Add the curry paste, ground ginger, and red pepper.

5. Stir to coat the onion and garlic in spices.

6. Pour in the diced tomatoes with their liquid, coconut milk, veggie broth, and lentils.

7. Stir before closing and sealing the lid.

8. Hit "manual" and cook for 6 minutes on high pressure.

9. When time is up, hit "cancel" and wait for the pressure to come down on its own.

10. When the pressure it all gone, throw in the spinach and serve when the leaves have wilted.

Nutritional Info (¼ recipe):

Total calories: 553
Protein: 22
Carbs: 60
Fiber: 7
Fat: 24

Weeknight Three-Bean Chili (Oil Free)

Serves: 6-8

Time: 26 minutes (10 minutes prep time, 6 minutes cook time, 10 minutes natural release)

This is probably one of the easiest and fastest chili recipes you could make. By using canned beans, you negate the need for soak time, and cut the cooking time in half. The result is a protein and fiber-hearty meal with lot of aromatics and spice.

Ingredients:

3 ½ cups veggie broth
1 can black beans
1 can red beans

1 can pinto beans

1, 14.5-ounce can diced tomatoes
1, 14.5-ounce can tomato sauce

2 cups chopped onion

¾ cup chopped carrots
¼ cup chopped celery

1 chopped red bell pepper

2 tablespoons mild chili powder

1 tablespoon minced garlic
1 ½ teaspoons ground cumin
1 ½ teaspoons dried oregano
1 teaspoon smoked paprika

Directions:

1. Rinse and drain the canned beans.

2. Heat your pressure cooker before throwing in the onion and garlic to sauté for 5 minutes or so.

3. Add the rest of the ingredients, except the tomatoes and tomato sauce.

4. Stir.

5. Close and seal the lid.

6. Select "manual" and cook on high pressure for 6 minutes.

7. When time is up, hit "cancel" and let the pressure come down naturally.

8. When the pressure is gone, stir in the tomato sauce and diced tomatoes.

9. If you want a thicker chili, spoon out 1-2 cups of the chili and blend before returning to the pot.

10. Serve with fresh parsley if desired.

Nutritional Info (⅛ recipe):

Total calories: 167
Protein: 10 Carbs: 32
Fiber: 11.5
Fat: 1

Root Veggie Soup

Serves: 8

Time: 1 hour, 30 minutes (10 minutes prep time, 30 minutes cook time, 50

minutes natural release)

Veggies from beneath the ground are very healthy. The vegetables of choice in this soup are potatoes, carrots, and onions. There's also some canned tomatoes and seasonings, of course, but the true stars are those nutritionpacked root vegetables.

Ingredients:

7 cups veggie broth
6 cups peeled and chopped russet potatoes
3 cups peeled and chopped carrots
1 cup Italian-style tomatoes (canned)

1 cup chopped yellow onion

½ cup coconut oil

2 tablespoons garlic powder

1 tablespoon mild chili powder
1 tablespoon salt

Directions:

1. Pour everything in your pressure cooker.

2. Stir before closing and sealing the lid.

3. Select "Soup" and adjust time to 30 minutes.

4. When time is up, hit "cancel" and wait for a natural pressure release.

5. To make the soup creamy, blend until smooth.

6. Taste and season more if necessary.

Nutritional Info (⅛ recipe):

Total calories: 256
Protein: 4
Carbs: 31
Fiber: 4
Fat: 14

Spicy Chili w/ Red Lentils (Oil Free)

Serves: 5

Time: 47 minutes (15 minutes prep time, 17 minutes cook time, 15 minutes natural release)

We can't get enough of red lentils! In this recipe, they're part of a spicy chili with just a hint of sweetness from some brown sugar and apple cider vinegar. The heat comes from a combination of cayenne, paprika, and chili powder.
To make this a full meal that can serve 4-5, serve over rice.

Ingredients:

7 cups water
2 cups red lentils
2 diced red peppers
1 diced onion
14-ounce can of diced tomatoes
5 minced garlic cloves
¼ cup brown sugar
6-ounce can of tomato paste
2 tablespoons apple cider vinegar
1 tablespoon paprika
1 tablespoon chili powder
1 teaspoon cayenne

Directions:

1. Prep your ingredients.

2. Throw everything in the pressure cooker and seal the lid.

3. Select "manual" and cook for 17 minutes on high pressure.

4. When the timer beeps, hit "cancel" and wait 15 minutes before quickreleasing.

5. Stir and serve over rice!

Nutritional Info (⅕ recipe, just chili):

Total calories: 420
Protein: 24
Carbs: 76
Fiber: 6
Fat: 2

Guacamole Soup (Oil Free)

Serves: 4

Time: 35 minutes (10 minutes prep time, 10 minutes cook time, 15 minutes natural release)

Creamy and warm, this avocado-based soup is the perfect accompaniment to some high-quality, crusty bread. Since avocados are relatively bland, the sweetness from the agave syrup, spiciness of the habanero, and earthiness of the cumin add layer upon layer of flavor.

Ingredients:

4 cups veggie stock
3 smashed, ripe avocados
1 chopped onion
3 minced garlic cloves
1 tablespoon ground cumin
1 bay leaf

1 teaspoon oregano

⅛ seeded and chopped small habanero
1-2
teaspoo
ns agave
syrup
Salt and
pepper
to taste

Directions:

1. Turn your pressure cooker to "sauté."

2. When hot, cook the onions and garlic for about 5 minutes, or until fragrant, and the onions are clear.

3. Add the rest of the ingredients (minus the agave) to the pot.

4. Select "manual," and cook on high pressure for 10 minutes.

5. When done, hit "cancel" and wait for the pressure to come down by itself.

6. When all the pressure is gone, open the lid and pick out the bay leaf.

7. Blend the soup till smooth before adding the agave syrup and a squirt of lime juice.

8. Season more to taste if necessary before serving.

Nutritional Info (¼ recipe):

Total calories: 239
Protein: 3
Carbs: 18
Fiber: 10
Fat: 17

"Meaty" Seitan Stew

Serves: 6-8

Time: 10 minutes

You learned how to make seitan back in the "One-Pot" chapter, and this recipe teaches you how to whip up a hearty stew with a seitan roast. With potatoes, carrots, corn, and green beans, it's a vegan version of a meaty classic.

Ingredients:

4 cups veggie broth
2 cups cubed seitan
6 quartered baby potatoes
3 chopped carrots
1, 15-ounce can of corn
1, 15-ounce can of green beans
1 chopped sweet onion

2 bay leaves

2 tablespoons vegan-friendly Worcestershire sauce
2 tablespoons arrowroot powder
1 tablespoon tomato paste
1 tablespoon cumin
1 teaspoon garlic powder 1 teaspoon onion powder
1 teaspoon paprika

Directions:

1. Dissolve the arrowroot powder in a little bit of water.
2. Pour (along with everything else) in the pressure cooker and stir.
3. Close and seal the lid.
4. Select "manual," and cook on high pressure for 10 minutes.
5. When the timer beeps, press "cancel" and then quick-release.
6. Pick out the bay leaves before serving.
7. Add some black pepper if desired.

Nutritional Info (⅛ recipe):

Total calories: 213
Protein: 19
Carbs: 29
Fiber: 3
Fat: 2

Classic (Vegan) Chili

Serves: 8

Time: 37 minutes (30 minutes prep time, 7 minutes cook time)

If you need a big hearty meal for a lot of people, this vegan chili is the perfect recipe. It's vegan-friendly while still being accessible to non-vegans, and if there are leftovers, it freezes really well. It's also incredibly quick at just under 40 minutes, so you don't need to spend all day cooking.

Ingredients:

6 cups tomato juice

7 cups canned kidney beans

2 cups textured soy protein (Bob's Red Mill)
2 cans diced tomatoes
1 cup water
5 minced garlic cloves

1 diced onion

2 tablespoons veggie oil

1 tablespoon + 1 teaspoon chili powder
1 teaspoon garlic powder
1 teaspoon sea salt
½ teaspoon cumin
Salt to taste

Directions:

Turn your pressure cooker to "sauté" and heat the veggie oil.

When hot, cook onions until they're soft and about to become clear.

3. Add the garlic and cook for a minute or so.

4. Scoop out the onions and garlic.

5. Add the tomato juice and seasonings.

6. Puree the onion/garlic mixture before returning to the pot.

7. Add the rest of the ingredients.

8. Close and seal the lid.

9. Hit "soup" and adjust time to 7 minutes.

10. When time is up, hit "cancel" and quick-release.

11. Taste and season before serving!

Nutritional Info (⅛ recipe):

Total calories: 331
Protein: 25
Carbs: 51
Fiber: 12
Fat: 5

Creamy Broccoli Soup with "Chicken" and Rice

Serves: 8-10
Time: 36 minutes (30 minutes prep time, 6 minutes cook time)

This soup uses a lot of vegan versions of ingredients, like vegan chicken and a bouillon cube. Some good brands include Beyond Meat, Better Than Bouillon, Edward & Sons, and Orrington Farms. You add the chicken and rice after pureeing the broccoli-and-cauliflower soup, so there's some texture.

Ingredients:

2 boxes of mushroom broth
2 bunches' worth of broccoli florets
1 head's worth of cauliflower florets

1 medium-sized, diced Yukon Gold potato

2 cups cooked brown rice

1 package of vegan chicken strips
1 vegan, chicken-flavored bouillon cube
1 cup water
1 cup unsweetened almond milk
3 minced garlic cloves

1 diced white onion

2 tablespoons tamari

1 tablespoon veggie oil
Dash of salt
Dash of black pepper

Directions:

Heat the oil in your pressure cooker on the "sauté" setting.

Toss in the onion and cook until soft.

3. Add garlic and cook for another minute or so.

4. Hit "cancel" and add the broccoli, cauliflower, and potato.

5. Season with the tamari, salt, pepper, and bouillon cube.

6. Pour in the liquids (water, milk, and broth) and stir.

7. Close and seal the lid.

8. Select "manual," and adjust time to 6 minutes on high pressure.

9. After hitting "cancel" when time is up, quick-release the pressure.

10. Puree when the soup has cooled a little.

11. Before serving, add the vegan chicken strips and cooked rice.

Nutritional Info (1/10 recipe):

Total calories: 193
Protein: 8
Carbs: 28
Fiber: 5
Fat: 5

Chicken(less) Soup (Oil Free)

Serves: 4

Time: 20 minutes (10 minutes prep time, 10 minutes cook time)

Craving chicken soup? You can get the flavor of chicken using tofu and a seasoning blend full of spices usually paired with poultry. The hot and comforting dish only takes 10 minutes under pressure followed by a quickrelease, so you can get your fix in a flash.

Ingredients:

6 cups hot water

1 cup diced potatoes

2 diced carrots

1 minced onion

1 diced celery rib

¾ cup cubed, extra-firm tofu

2 bay leaves

2 tablespoons seasoning blend*
2 teaspoons minced garlic
1 teaspoon salt
⅛ teaspoon dried thyme
*¾ cup nutritional yeast flakes
1 ½ tablespoons onion powder
1 tablespoon dried basil
1 tablespoon dried oregano
1 tablespoon dried parsley
1 teaspoon salt
½ teaspoon celery seed
¼ teaspoon white pepper

Cooking Tip: You can use your seasoning blend for any dish that requires a chicken-like flavor! About ½ tablespoon per 1 cup of hot water will produce a good flavor.

Directions:

1. To make your seasoning blend, put everything in a blender and process until it has become a fine powder. Don't breathe it in.

2. Mix 2 tablespoons into your water and set aside.

3. Turn your pressure cooker to "sauté" and cook the onion until brown.

4. Add garlic and cook for another minute.

5. Add the rest of the ingredients, including the seasoned water.

6. Close and seal the lid.

7. Select "soup" and adjust time to 10 minutes.

8. When time is up, hit "cancel" to turn off the cooker, and then quickrelease.

9. Serve!

Nutritional Info (¼ recipe):

Total calories: 90
Protein: 6
Carbs: 15
Fiber: 3
Fat: 2

Fava Bean Dip

Makes: 1 ½ cups
Time: 27 minutes (5 minutes prep time, 12 minutes cook time, 10 minutes natural release) + overnight bean soak

Homemade bean dip is very easy and delicious with fresh-cut veggies, pita, or pita chips. This recipe produces 1 ½ cups, so make this for you and a movie-night buddy to share. Keep in mind that you'll need to soak the beans overnight before using the pressure cooker.

Ingredients:

3 cups water
2 cups soaked split fava beans
2 crushed garlic cloves
2 tablespoons veggie oil
1 tablespoon olive oil

1 zested and juiced lemon

2 teaspoons tahini

2 teaspoons cumin
1 teaspoon harissa
1 teaspoon paprika Salt to taste

Directions:

1. The night before, soak the fava beans and drain the fava beans before beginning the recipe.

2. Preheat your pressure cooker.

3. Add garlic when hot and cook until they become golden.

4. Add beans, veggie oil, and 3 cups of water.

5. Close and seal the lid.

6. Select "manual" and cook on high pressure for 12 minutes.

7. When time is up, hit "cancel" and wait 10 minutes before quickreleasing any remaining pressure.

8. Drain the cooking liquid from the pressure cooker, leaving about 1 cup.

9. Toss in the tahini, cumin, harissa, and lemon zest.

10. Puree until smooth.

11. Salt and blend again.

12. Serve with a drizzle of olive oil and dash of paprika.

Nutritional Info (½ recipe):

Total calories: 415
Protein: 15
Carbs: 31
Fiber: 7
Fat: 26

Mango Chutney

Makes: 2 cups
Time: 25 minutes (5 minutes prep time, 20 minutes cook time)

Mango chutney is a spicy-sweet condiment that can be used in everything from curries to sandwiches with avocado and alfalfa sprouts. It would also be awesome on a veggie burger!

Cooking Tip: Refrigerated chutney will last up to a month, while in the freezer, it can last up to a year.

Ingredients:

2 big, diced mangos
1 cored and diced apple
1 ¼ cups apple cider vinegar
1 ¼ cups raw sugar
¼ cup raisins

1 chopped shallot

2 tablespoons finely-diced ginger

1 tablespoon veggie oil

2 teaspoons salt

½ teaspoon red pepper flakes
¼ teaspoon cardamom powder
⅛ teaspoons cinnamon

Directions:

1   Preheat your pressure cooker.

2   When hot, add the oil and cook shallots and ginger until the shallot is soft.

3   Add cinnamon, chili powder, and cardamom and cook for 1 minute.

4   Add the rest of the ingredients and mix.

5   When the sugar has melted, close and seal the lid.

6   Select "manual" and cook for 7 minutes on high pressure.

7   When the beeper sounds, hit "cancel" and wait for the pressure to come down on its own.

8   Turn the pot back to "sauté" with the lid off until the chutney has a jam-like texture.

9   When it starts to thicken, turn the cooker to the "keep warm" setting.

10 When you get the texture you want, move the chutney to glass jars and close.

11 When the contents are cool, move to the fridge.

Nutritional Info (1 tablespoon):

Total calories: 78.2
Protein: .9
Carbs: 18.3
Fiber: 1
Fat: .3

Mushroom Risotto

Serves: 4-6

Time: 30 minutes (10 minutes prep time, 20 minutes cook time)

Rich roasted mushrooms, vegan butter, and umami miso paste make for one delicious risotto. It's so good and satisfying you could eat this as a main course if you wanted, though a small amount as a side dish with stuffed eggplant would also be good.

Ingredients:

4 cups veggie stock
1 ½ pounds mixed, chopped mushrooms
1 ounce dried porcini mushrooms

2 cups Arborio rice

1 cup chopped yellow onion
¾ cups dry white wine
4 tablespoons olive oil
4 tablespoons vegan butter

1 tablespoon miso paste

2 teaspoons soy sauce

2   teaspoons minced garlic
½ cup chopped herbs

Directions:

1.   Microwave the dried mushrooms in broth for 5 minutes.

2.   Chop the porcini and set aside for now. Keep the broth separate.

3   Heat olive oil in your pressure cooker.

4   Add the fresh mixed mushrooms and cook for about 8 minutes until brown.

5.   Season with salt and pepper.

6.   Add the onion, garlic, porcini, and butter.

7.   Stir until the onions are soft.

8.   Add the rice and stir to coat in oil.

9.   When toasty after 3-4 minutes, add the soy sauce and miso paste.

10.   Pour in the wine and cook for 2 minutes.

11.   Pour the broth through a strainer into the pot and deglaze.

12.   Close and seal the pressure cooker.

13.   Select "manual" and cook on high pressure for 5 minutes.

14.   When the beeper goes off, hit "cancel" and quick-release.

15.   Open the lid and stir. If it's not thick enough, turn on the "sauté" program and stir.

16.   Add herbs and season with salt and pepper before serving.

Nutritional Info (⅙ recipe):

Total calories: 431
Protein: 10
Carbs: 58
Fiber: 8
Fat: 17

Smoky Lima Beans

Serves: 12

Time: 1 hour, 10 minutes (25 minutes cook time, 5 minutes natural pressure release, 10 minutes boil time, 20-30 minutes simmer time)

For smoky, campfire-ready lima beans, all you need is the right seasonings. No meat at all. For the liquid smoke, Colgin is a good vegan brand, but most brands should be vegan. Just take a look at the ingredient list to be sure. To make enough beans for 12 people, you'll need an 8-quart cooker.

Ingredients:

12 cups water
2 pounds dry large lima beans
⅛ cup Colgin liquid smoke
1 teaspoon onion powder
 1 teaspoon garlic powder
Salt and pepper to taste

Directions:

1. Rinse beans before putting into the pressure cooker with your water.

2. Add onion and garlic powder, and seal the lid.

3. Hit "Bean" and adjust to 25 minutes.

4. When time is up, wait 5 minutes and then quick-release the pressure.

5. Add salt and liquid smoke.

6. Taste and add more seasonings if necessary.

7. Hit "sauté" and bring to a boil for 10 minutes.

8. Then, hit "cancel."

9. Turn back to "sauté" and simmer for 20-30 minutes, until thickened.

Nutritional Info (½ cup per serving):

Total calories: 213
Protein: 16
Carbs: 40
Fat: 0
Fiber: 7

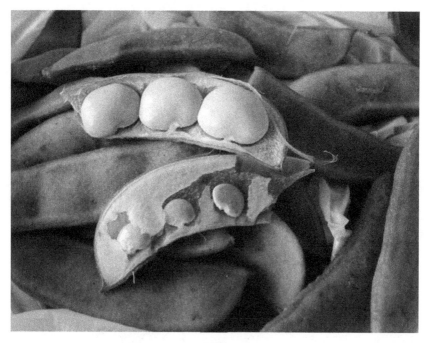

Polenta with Herbs (Oil Free)

Serves: 4-6

Time: 20 minutes (5 minutes prep time, 5 minutes cook time, 10 minutes natural release)

Polenta can be tricky to get just right, but it's easy when you use the pressure cooker. This is a simple recipe with simple, rustic flavors coming from lots of fresh herbs, onion, and garlic. You can use dried; just remember to reduce the amount by about half, since dried herbs have more concentrated flavor.

Ingredients:

3 cups veggie broth

1 cup water

1 cup coarse-ground polenta

1 large minced onion

3 tablespoons fresh, chopped thyme

2 tablespoons fresh, chopped Italian parsley

1 tablespoon minced garlic

1 teaspoon fresh, chopped sage

Salt and pepper to taste

Directions:

1. Preheat your cooker and dry-sautè the onion for about a minute.

2. Add the minced garlic and cook for one more minute.

3. Pour in the broth, along with the thyme, parsley, and sage.

4. Stir.

5. Sprinkle the polenta in the pot, but don't stir it in.

6. Close and seal the lid.

7. Select "manual" and cook on high pressure for 5 minutes.

8. When the timer beeps, hit "cancel" and wait 10 minutes.

9. Pick out the bay leaf.

10. Using a whisk, stir the polenta to smooth it. If it's thin, simmer on the "sauté" setting until it reaches the consistency you like.

11. Season to taste with salt and pepper before serving.

Nutritional Info (⅙ recipe):

Total calories: 103

Protein: 0

Carbs: 3

Fat: 0

Fiber: 2

Sweet Thai Coconut Rice (Oil Free)

Serves: 4

Time: About 23 minutes (3 minutes cook time, 10 minutes natural release, 510 minutes rest time)

This 5-ingredient side dish can be easily adapted into a dessert by adding more sugar, but it also makes a tasty afternoon snack when you're craving something a little sweet.

Ingredients:

1 ½ cups water
1 cup Thai sweet rice
½ can full-fat coconut milk
2 tablespoons sugar
Dash of salt

Directions:

1. Mix rice and water in your pressure cooker.

2. Select "manual" and cook for just 3 minutes on high pressure.

3. When time is up, hit "cancel" and wait 10 minutes for a natural release.

4. In the meanwhile, heat coconut milk, sugar, and salt in a saucepan.

5. When the sugar has melted, remove from the heat.

6. When the cooker has released its pressure, mix the coconut milk mixture into your rice and stir.

7. Put the lid back on and let it rest 5-10 minutes, without returning it to pressure.

---

8.   Serve and enjoy!

Nutritional Info (¼ recipe):

Total calories: 269
Protein: 4
Carbs: 47
Fiber: 0
Fat: 8

Porcini Mushroom Pate

Serves: 6-8

Time: 2 hours, 21 minutes (10 minutes prep time, 11 minutes cook time, 2 hours chill time)

Pate is traditionally made with very fatty meat, which is a big no-no for vegans for a variety of reasons. "True" pate is even illegal in many countries because of animal cruelty laws. Luckily, there's none of that going on in this recipe. You use both fresh and dried mushrooms for a rich, earthy spread seasoned simply with shallot, salt, pepper, and a bay leaf.

Ingredients:

1 pound sliced fresh cremini mushrooms
30 grams rinsed dry porcini mushrooms
1 cup boiling water
¼ cup dry white wine
1 bay leaf

1 sliced shallot

2 tablespoons olive oil

3 1 ½ teaspoons salt ½ teaspoon white pepper

Directions:

1. Place dry porcini mushrooms in a bowl and pour over boiling water.

2. Cover and set aside for now.

3. Heat 1 tablespoon of oil in your pressure cooker.

4. When hot, cook the shallot until soft.

5. Add cremini mushrooms and cook until they've turned golden.

6. Deglaze with the wine, and let it evaporate.

7. Pour in the porcini mushrooms along with their water.

8. Toss in salt, pepper, and the bay leaf.

9. Close and seal the lid.

10. Select "manual" and cook on high pressure for 10 minutes.

11. When the timer beeps, hit "cancel" and quick-release.

12. Pick out the bay leaf before adding the last tablespoon of oil.

13. Puree mixture until smooth.

14. Refrigerate in a closed container for at least 2 hours before eating.

Nutritional Info (⅛ recipe):

Total calories: 70
Protein: 4 Carbs: 6
Fiber: 2.6
Fat: 4

Japanese-Pumpkin Rice

Serves: 2-4

Time: 22 minutes (5 minutes prep time, 7 minutes cook time, 10 minutes natural release)

This unique rice dish is so easy to make. There's no sautéing or multiple cooking steps, you literally just put everything in your pressure cooker, cook, and eat! Japanese pumpkin is known in America as Kabocha squash. It's basically a cross between the sweetness of a pumpkin and a sweet potato.

Ingredients:

2 cups cubed Kabocha squash
2 cups (360 ml) rice
1 ½ cups water
4 drops sesame oil
1 tablespoon cooking sake
1 teaspoon salt

Directions:

1. Mix rice, water, sake, sesame oil, and salt in your pressure cooker.

2. Add the squash.

3. Close and seal the lid.

4. Select "manual," and cook on high pressure for 7 minutes.

5. When time is up, hit "cancel" and wait 10 minutes.

6. Quick-release any remaining pressure.

7. Stir and serve!

Nutritional Info (¼ recipe):

Total calories: 355
Protein: 9
Carbs: 82
Fiber: 6
Fat:

Conclusion

I hope that this book has inspired you to try out more vegan recipes, even if you aren't a vegan or are still in the transitional phase where you're adding food, and not eliminating just yet. Being a vegan does not mean sacrificing quality or diversity when it comes to food, so don't let anyone discourage you with comments about how you're "missing out."

A pressure cooker is the must-have tool for vegans. This book covered how to use the cooker, how to keep it clean and well-maintained, and provided cooking charts on the most common ingredients you'll be using as a vegan. Whether you're making beans, lentils, pasta, oats, veggies, or fruit, the pressure cooker is significantly faster than any other cooking method, and preserves the most nutrition. It's a double-win.

Your health should be a top priority. When you're in good health, everything else is easier. Vegan food prepared with a pressure cooker is the single best way to improve your health without complicating your life. Please come back to this book and its awesome recipes again and again to continue your vegan journey. I love walking alongside you.

CPSIA information can be obtained
at www.ICGtesting.com
Printed in the USA
BVHW061223010321
601386BV00001B/152